GEORGE ELIOT
from a chalk drawing of 1865 by F. W. BURTON
National Portrait Gallery

GEORGE ELIOT

by

LETTICE COOPER

PUBLISHED FOR
THE BRITISH COUNCIL
BY LONGMAN GROUP LTD

LONGMAN GROUP LTD
Longman House, Burnt Mill, Harlow, Essex

*Associated companies, branches and
representatives throughout the world*

*First published 1951
Revised editions 1960, 1970
Reprinted with additions to Bibliography 1966,*
© Lettice Cooper 1960, 1970

*Printed in Great Britain by
F. Mildner & Sons, London, EC1*

SBN O 582 01015 2

GEORGE ELIOT

I. MARIAN EVANS

IN the midlands of England, between the manufacturing
towns of Coventry and Nuneaton, lies a stretch of level
country, undramatic, without mountain or river. The
soil is rich, it is farmers' country, but even in the first half
of the nineteenth century, when one coach a day linked
Coventry with Nuneaton, it was partly industrial. The
manor house looked across the green plain to the colliery
tip; the villager, who wove cloth on the handloom in his
cottage, carried it to be finished at the neighbouring mill.
But it was mostly rural with Shakespeare's birthplace only a
few miles away, a countryside of red brick farms, of cow-
slips and cuckoos, of wide skies reflected in canal waters.
In this country, in 1819, Mary Ann, or Marian, Evans, later
to be George Eliot, was born.

Her father, Robert Evans, Welsh by descent, was the son
of a builder and carpenter. He started his working life as a
farmer, but later became agent for the estate of Arbury, the
property of a Warwickshire landowner. Evans was a man
known and respected throughout the county, both for his
upright character, and for his wide knowledge of the whole
fabric of country life. He could give sound advice about
house or farm buildings, about timber, mining, soil, land
valuation, stock, or crops. He was traditional in his
opinions, a life-long supporter of the Church of England
and of the Tory party. Marian was his youngest child, the
third child of his second marriage, to the daughter of a
yeoman farmer. When Marian was born, the two children
of the first marriage were nearly grown up, and soon
moved out into the world. Her parents, her sister Christiana,
and her brother, Isaac, made up her home.

The youngest child in such a family sometimes feels
anxiously that there is no one left for her. Father and

3

mother have each other, brother and sister are already allies. The passionate longing for someone of her own, someone to put her first was to run all through George Eliot's life, and it was not until she found it in George Henry Lewes that her genius was to flower. The child, Marian, craved above all for the whole love of her brother, Isaac. Naturally she was disappointed, for Issac at eight years old went to school, returning only for the holidays from the world of boys and men to pet and patronize the little sister with whom he was often impatient. She could not walk far enough nor climb high enough, she cried too easily, and her devouring affection set up the inevitable resistance. There was plenty of kindness in the family for Marian, her father was especially fond of her, but there was no one to be hers alone. The high-powered child in the household of ordinary people suffered the disproportionate agonies of her kind.

There were minor troubles, Marian was plain and untidy ; her sister, Chrissey, was pretty and neat. Chrissey was the favourite with the grown-up people, a good girl, useful in the house, and approved by their mother, while Marian was often in disgrace for slouching over a book instead of helping, and for her unmanageable mane of hair. Not that she was always unhappy. It was a good life for a child in the red brick house at Griff, with its farm buildings, garden, and pond, and with the freedom of wood and field all round. Her father often took her with him as he drove about the Arbury estate. Standing between his knees in farm or cottage as he sat and discussed the tenants' problems, Marian absorbed a great deal about country people and their lives. Those years of childhood, she said in one of her unremarkable poems, were 'seed to all my good', and she speaks of 'blest hours of infantine content'. She was, in fact, like most children, sometimes unhappy and sometimes happy, but both with more intensity than most children because she was a woman on a grand scale in the making.

Mrs Evans was delicate, and to relieve her the two girls

were sent early away to school, first to a small school at Attleborough in Warwickshire, where Marian suffered from the cold and from night terrors; next to a larger school at Nuneaton. Miss Lewis, the first mistress here, became Marian's great friend, and later, it was to her that the girl wrote those ponderous, priggish, pathetic letters that were her chief outlet between the ages of seventeen and twenty-five. Miss Lewis was caught up in the full tide of the Evangelical Movement, which in its later stages was to break away from the Established Church of England into Nonconformity, but in its early stages was a movement within the Established Church, and did much to re-animate a more personal and vital faith. Marian, in adolescence, was strongly influenced by Miss Lewis. Her temperament was deeply religious and goodness was always to be her predominant interest in life. When Marian was fifteen, her mother died, and soon afterwards Chrissey married. Marian left school and took charge of the house and of her father and brother. She also visited the poor, and did her share of work at the Clothing Clubs and other charities of the neighbourhood. The solemn sixteen-year-old went gravely through these boring duties with the older women, secretly panting for a richer life, and for a chance to use the full powers of which she was conscious. 'You may try, but you cannot imagine what it is to have a man's force of genius in you, yet to suffer the slavery of being a girl.'

Some life of her own she did have. She took lessons in Italian, German, and music. She read as always, greedily, but there was no one to whom she could talk about books and ideas. Miss Lewis by post was her nearest approach to congenial company. Her deep-rooted sense of duty and the strong Puritanism which in early life exalted the value of self-sacrifice prevented Marian from contemplating any change. Her father lived at Griff, and it was her duty to look after her father. No doubt there were many afternoons when she walked alone by the canal, and saw her life as an interminable round of duty and self-sacrifice. Years

afterwards, when asked if she would ever write her auto-
biography, she said of that time: 'The only thing that I
should care to dwell on would be the absolute despair I
suffered of ever being able to achieve anything.' At this
time in her life she was not even able to enjoy an occasional
holiday, for when at nineteen she paid a first visit to London
with her brother, Isaac, she refused to go to a theatre, and
wrote austerely to Miss Lewis: 'I was not at all delighted
with the stir of the Great Babel.' Miss Lewis's Evangelicalism
had done its work. Just before her nineteenth birthday,
Marian wrote, 'May I seek to be sanctified wholly!' A
provincial young prig? Yes, but a chrysalis, in whom life
and colour and winged power were the more closely folded
because the colours were unusually bright and the wings
strong. They were soon to begin breaking their sheath.

To a great many artists who have struggled out of a
society indifferent to the arts, the first congenial friendship
has been the opening of the new world. When Marian
was twenty-two, Isaac married, and took over from his
father both the agency for the Arbury estate and the agent's
house at Griff. Robert Evans and Marian moved to a semi-
detached house in Foleshill Road, Coventry. Coventry
was then a small town, but it was the country girl's first
entry into the great world. Here for the first time she made
friends who shared her own interests, Charles Bray, whose
book, *The Philosophy of Necessity* was published in that year;
his wife, Sara, formerly Sara Hennell, whose brother Charles
had written *An Inquiry Concerning the Origin of Christianity*
which Marian had already read. It must have been delight-
ful to the bookish girl to meet authors in the flesh, to
go for the first time to a house where free discussion of
abstract ideas was the natural climate. To the new friends
Marian seemed a gentle, modest girl who surprised them
by the wide range of her reading and by everything that
distinguished her from the more commonplace young
women of the neighbourhood. She was not pretty. Her
head was large, her face heavy, she had no self-confidence,

believing herself to be plainer than she really was, for her eyes were beautiful, and there was great sweetness in her voice and smile. She had no surface charm and was not easy to know, but there was a warmth and sincerity in her that made her lovable to anyone who could break the barrier of diffidence.

The evangelical Miss Lewis must have felt that she was losing her hold on her pupil, who had been questioning the tenets of orthodox religion for some time, even before she met the Brays. Stimulated by the constant discussion in their house, and encouraged by their moral support, she dramatically and solemnly renounced her faith. It was a shattering blow to her father, who even threatened to sell the house, and to go and live with his married daughter. Marian accepted the challenge. She would take lodgings in Coventry and earn her living by teaching. She went away for a few weeks. Common sense and the discovery that he was very uncomfortable without her prevailed with Robert Evans. He agreed to receive her again and she compromised by accompanying him to church on Sundays. She remained with him until he died, when she was thirty years old.

During this time she achieved her first piece of writing apart from her voluminous, and, it must be admitted, tedious letters. She translated Strauss's *Das Leben Jesu*. It took her two years and often bored her, but probably it helped to form the habit of sticking to a long piece of work which is so necessary for the writer of even the most inspired novel. This was a miserable time in her life, only relieved by her friendship with the Brays and Hennells. Her father, in his failing health, often could not bear to be left alone for an hour. Her own health suffered from the confined life and from the day-long frustration of her urgent spirit, which had not yet found its proper channels. She loved her father deeply and his feebleness and approaching death tore her heart. 'What shall I be without my father? It will seem as if a part of my moral nature was gone!' Clearly if she was to develop her full powers she needed more freedom to develop in her own way, and her friends must have been relieved for her when after his long illness Robert Evans died. The Brays were just going abroad for a holiday. They took Marian with them, and left her in a *pension* at Geneva, where she spent a peaceful eight months, a time for readjustment and rest.

When she came back to England, she met at the Brays' house John Chapman, who had just become editor of the *Westminster Review*. He gave her some books to review. A little later on, he bought the paper, and offered her the post of honorary assistant editor. She was to be paid for her contributions, and she had a small income of her own. She came up to London, lodged with the Chapmans, and settled in to work on the paper.

The work delighted her but there was soon trouble at home. Chapman's wife grew jealous of her. His relationship with Marian, although they were never lovers, was warm, based on shared interests, and touched with enough feeling to make it extremely stimulating to both of them. Chapman was at that time having an affair with the children's governess, a pretty, silly girl, who also lived in the house, and whom Mrs Chapman seems to have tolerated. Wife and mistress combined to drive out Marian. Indignant, she returned to Coventry, and the *Westminster Review* immediately fell into disorder without her energy and ability. Chapman went after her, and persuaded his wife and mistress to agree that she should come back. Surprisingly she came. She had already travelled a long way from the evangelical girl at Griff. She lived two years in Chapman's house and, in the constant stir of work and interesting society, the three women managed somehow to live together in comparative peace while Chapman no doubt enjoyed the best of all three worlds.

Marian was now in the full tide of London literary life. She met Dickens and Froude and Huxley, Harriet Martineau, Grote, and J. S. Mill. She became a great friend of the philosopher, Herbert Spencer. He was near her own age, handsome and distinguished, sharing all her interests. It was one of those friendships that everybody expected to ripen into marriage, but this never happened. Spencer had theories about marriage, he thought the legal bond between two people incompatible with perfect happiness. Probably he was rationalizing a deep-rooted fear, but his views may have influenced Marian and prepared the way for her union with George Lewes. Spencer's influence was very important in another way, for it was he who first suggested to her that she might try her hand at fiction.

Herbert Spencer introduced Lewes to Marian. Lewes was at that time editing the *Leader*, the first critical weekly to appear in England. He was an ugly, lively, genial, amusing, warm-hearted man, a very high-class journalist, who did not hesitate to tackle any subject, and had something stimulating if not profound to say about most of them. He was a brilliant editor, the kind of man who promotes good work in other people. He was unhappily married; his young wife had been seduced by Thornton Hunt, son of Leigh Hunt. Thornton Hunt was the father of two of the children who bore the name of Lewes. Under the law as it then stood, Lewes could not get a divorce. He made his wife and children an allowance and lived apart from her.

Marian and Lewes fell deeply in love, and she had to make a choice on which her whole life was to depend. Her father's strict piety, her mother's yeoman pride, her country and small town respectability, even her friends at Coventry who a few years ago had seemed so daring, were on the side of self-denial, and she had grown up with self-denial as a religion. All her past was against an illegal union with Lewes, but life and love and the future were on his side. She agreed to live with him as his unmarried wife. In the summer of 1854, they went abroad together for what was in all but name a honeymoon.

It was not as she would have chosen it to be. She was sensitive to the good opinion of her friends and family; she had qualms then and afterwards. But at last she had a full emotional life, someone who needed her as she needed him, someone with whom she came first. Lewes's love and admiration were a continual reassurance against her diffidence. She was no longer lonely. From the fulfilment of her nature came the release of her pen. Marian, who would have preferred to be Marian Lewes, was still Marian Evans, but she was to have a new name which was to obliterate both. Soon after they returned to England, she began her career as a novelist under the pen-name of George Eliot.

II. GEORGE ELIOT

Scenes of Clerical Life

Marian and George Lewes settled down in a small house at Richmond. It was necessary for both to go on working, there were Lewes's wife and children to provide for as well as themselves. Marian had often dreamed of writing a novel. Now, under the stimulus of happy love and of discriminating encouragement the idea came to birth. She began with a long-short story, 'Amos Barton', which appeared in *Blackwood's Magazine* under the pen-name of George Eliot, chosen because George was the name of her beloved, and she liked the sound of Eliot. *Blackwood's* also published the two stories which followed, 'Mr Gilfil's Love Story', and 'Janet's Repentance'. The three of them appeared together, in 1858, in book form under the title of *Scenes of Clerical Life*. Even while the stories were appearing separately, they arrested attention, and were at once recognized, among others by Dickens and Thackeray, as the work of a new writer of importance.

It was the hey-day of Victorian fiction. Thackeray's *The Virginians* was running in serial form, as well as Dickens's *Little Dorrit*, and *A Tale of Two Cities* was to appear in 1859.

It was ten years since the publication of *Wuthering Heights*, Charlotte Brontë's *Villette* had appeared in 1853, Dickens, Thackeray, the Brontës, all were novelists of heightened tone and colour. By comparison with them George Eliot was sober, rooted in everyday life. She used for her three scenes the three backgrounds of her youth and childhood, the country parish with its village and surrounding farms; the great country house which she knew so well from her father's long connexion with Arbury; the country town like Coventry, which served her as a setting for the clash between the new Evangelical Movement in the Church and the traditional religion.

George Eliot came late to her vocation. She was thirty-eight when she wrote *Scenes of Clerical Life*, and the substance of nearly all her novels was to be memory, worked upon by her creative imagination. She always turned back for her material to the scenes of her first thirty years, and except for some parts of her last novel, *Daniel Deronda*, she wrote almost always about provincial life.

Her memory for the speech of the countryside was particularly acute. The Vicar, Amos Barton, struggling to keep wife and children on a miserably inadequate income, is presented to the reader by village gossip. The village sees that the simple, stupid man is deluded by the pinchbeck charms of the 'Countess', and that her stay at the Vicarage is an imposition which is going to prove the last straw to Milly Barton, worn out by her exertions and pregnant with yet another child. The village recognizes and exaggerates the spark of romantic feeling for the Countess which appears to Amos himself to be no more than good will towards a friend in trouble. Both the hard judgement of the Vicar's deluded innocence and the practical kindness when Milly is on her death-bed are the very essence of village life.

Milly herself is the first of George Eliot's notable women. Indeed the central figure in each scene of *Clerical Life* is a woman. Mr Gilfil is only there to tell the story, and presumably is a clergyman to provide the link with the other two tales. Any honest young lover and mourning husband would have done as well. It is Caterina's story. Caterina, the Italian-born adopted child of the great house, is the young Marian Evans, the girl whose intensity of feeling could find no adequate response in the more phlegmatic people round her. Caterina is separated from her surroundings by not being English, as Marian had felt herself isolated by a greater capacity for passion and suffering.

'Amos Barton', and 'Mr Gilfil's Love Story', although fairly long, are real short stories, given unity by one theme. 'Janet's Repentance' shows that already George Eliot is moving towards the form of the novel, for it is made up of two interweaving strands. Janet's miserable relationship with her husband, the deterioration of her character under the strain, and her redemption through the influence of the good, evangelical clergyman, Mr Tryan, is the main theme, but Mr Tryan's struggle against the ill-will and suspicion of the conservative townspeople is also important. The Evangelical movement, the clash between the old and new ways of ministry and worship in the Church, had always interested George Eliot. She had remarked in one of her earlier letters that it was a pity that English novelists neglected this subject which lay ready to their hand, and she continued to be interested in it long after she herself had abandoned any form of worship. Her admiration for the saintly characters that the movement produced colours especially her early novels, and Miss Lewis, even if she mourned for the pupil who had slipped away from her, must, if she was worldly enough to read novels at all, have realized that she had left her mark. Indeed it was so deep a mark that George Eliot could never handle her good evangelicals quite dispassionately. Mr Tryan, as later in *Adam Bede* Dinah Morris, seems a little too good to be true. He is even a trifle mawkish, and the sentimentality with which George Eliot handles him is the weakness of *Janet's Repentance*.

Its strength, as in the other two stories, is in the woman, in Janet herself. She is one of those women of great possibilities only partly realized, whom George Eliot was to develop in her later novels. Janet, brutally treated by her husband, drinks to escape from her sorrows. Such a heroine was a new departure in fiction. It is impossible to imagine Dickens or Thackeray allowing one of their good young women even to think of such a failing. Their good women were good and their bad women were bad, but George Eliot was already emerging from this tradition. 'If', she wrote, 'the ethics of art do not permit the truthful presentation of a character essentially noble, yet liable to great error that is anguish to its own nobleness, then it seems to me that the ethics of art are too narrow.' For her, and through her for the novel, they were already widening. Caterina who could contemplate murder, Janet who could take refuge from her sorrows in drunkenness, belong to the modern novel, which, it has lately been recognized, owes so much to George Eliot.

Henry James remarked that for George Eliot the novel was 'not primarily a picture of life but a moralized fable'. It is true that the problem of goodness, of how far people manage to live up to the best that is in them, gives an underlying urgency to all her work. But the picture of life is also there and emerges in these stories in a hundred touches of insight and descriptive power, even though parts of the stories are sentimentalized. It was clear to the readers of *Blackwood's* that here was a new author of great gifts. 'It is a long time', Blackwood wrote to his unknown contributor, 'since I have read anything so fresh, so humorous, so touching'. Always diffident, George Eliot throve on encouragement. Her first full-length novel, *Adam Bede*, appeared in 1859, only a year after *Scenes of Clerical Life* was published in book form.

Adam Bede

Dickens was one of the first to recognize that the new novelist was a woman and, by the time that *Adam Bede* was published, the authorship was no longer a secret, although

George Eliot continued to write under her pen name. The germ of *Adam Bede* was a story that she once heard from a Methodist aunt who had accompanied a condemned girl to the place of her execution. From this sprang the idea of Hetty Sorrel, condemned to death for the murder of her illegitimate child, and of Dinah Morris, the Methodist preacher who comforted Hetty in prison and went with her on her way to the scaffold. As in 'Janet's Repentance', George Eliot still sees Evangelicalism through the haze of her adolescent romance, and Dinah Morris, like Mr Tryan, is an idealized character, completely flawless. She is less irritating than Mr Tryan because, as with all her good women, George Eliot is very successful in giving an impression of real sweetness. Dinah is someone whom it is impossible wholly to accept, but also impossible to dislike. She may have been half-unconsciously modelled on Miss Lewis, but probably she had in her a good deal of the quality of her author.

The seed of the plot fell into rich soil. George Eliot told her publishers that her first full-length novel would be 'full of the breath of cows and the scent of hay'. The real substance of *Adam Bede* is all the country background of her youth. The Poysers' farm is in the centre of the canvas, presided over by Mrs Poyser, a figure whose earthy and homely reality makes Dinah Morris appear thin. Mrs Poyser was probably Marian's own mother, the daughter of a yeoman farmer, fragile of body, intrepid of spirit, with her shrewd tongue and her kind heart. Adam Bede himself derives from Marian's father, Robert Evans, the upright workman, self-respecting and generally respected for character and capacity. Adam suffers a little, like Dinah, from excess of virtue, although he is conscious of a hardness in himself which finally breaks down when he holds out his arm to Hetty in court. The reader turns with some relief to the imperfect characters, to the pretty, vain, childish Hetty, and to her seducer, the Squire's son, Arthur Donnithorne, who is not a deliberate villain, but a spoiled young man brought up to expect things to go easily for him, and appalled at the result of his pleasant dalliance.

The weakness of the book, beside the excessive virtue of Dinah, is, as with so many Victorian novels, the sacrifice of probability to plot and the tidiness of the ending. George Eliot was moving towards a new kind of novel in which representation of life was to be more important than the resolution of a plot, but she was still partly bound by the old convention. Hetty's pardon, so dramatically and improbably brought to the place of execution by Arthur Donnithorne, is an artificial device to spare the reader. In the relationship between Hetty and Arthur, and in all that grows out of it, there is a sense of destiny which is falsified by this resolution. Again, while Adam's love for Hetty is utterly convincing, and the thing that brings him most to life as a human being, his final marriage to Dinah, has none of that inevitability, but seems like a mechanical device to round off the story.

But these are the flaws in a rich tapestry of rural life of the time, the farm, the cottage, the workshop, the Rectory, the great house. It is a picture of a society based on the land, a society still stable, a hierarchy in which each order has its own rights. The scene in which Mrs Poyser routs the old Squire, who has come to propose a deal in farm property which would be unfair to them, has all the sturdy quality of an English folk song.

You may run away from my words, sir, and you may go spinnin' underhand ways o' doing us a mischief—for you've got Old Harry to your friend, though nobody else is—but I tell you for once as we're not dumb creatures to be abused and made money on by them as ha' got the lash i' their hands for want o' knowing how to undo the tackle. An' if I'm the only one who speaks my mind, there's plenty o' the same way of thinking i' this parish and the next to 't; for your name's no better than a brimstone match in everybody's nose—if it isna two-three old folks as you think o' saving your soul by giving 'em a bit o' flannel and a drop o' porridge. An' you may be right i' thinking it'll take but little to save your soul, for it'll be the smallest savin' y' ever made wi' all your scrapin'!

Such was the speech—witty, pungent, and coloured with homely images—that George Eliot heard in her childhood, and that was a great part of her training as a writer.

The Mill on the Floss

The life that Marian and George Lewes led together, at first in the house at Richmond, later in London in a house near Regent's Park, was one, as he recorded in his diary, of 'deep wedded happiness'. The stepsons were devoted to Marian, and she to them. Both Marian and Lewes worked hard and were always interested in each other's work, although inevitably, as her books appeared and her reputation soared, hers became the first consideration. Lewes was born to be an unselfish Prince Consort. Marian found in him the heart-whole devotion that she had always yearned for. He cherished her, cheered her melancholy, encouraged her diffidence, spared her the practical difficulties of life, entertained the people who came to their house, leaving Marian free for the only kind of social pleasure she liked, serious conversation with one or at most a few real friends. He even kept from her the few unfavourable reviews of her novels. It seems strange that a woman of her fibre should have allowed such a thing to happen, but she was abnormally sensitive and prone to melancholy and self-distrust. Except for these dark moods, and for bad headaches and other minor ailments which often troubled her, and except for a certain amount of anxiety about Lewes's never robust health, their life was extremely happy. George Eliot's career moved steadily from success to success as her great talent expanded. There is little to tell of the life that ran so smoothly, and George Eliot's history is the history of her novels from the time that she joined George Lewes up to his death.

Her second long novel, *The Mill on the Floss*, was published in 1860, only a year after *Adam Bede*. It was the book in which she drew most directly on her own early life. Maggie Tulliver, the sensitive, passionate child of a stolid family, craving for her brother's love, the ardent girl growing up in a narrow world with a thirst for life, beauty, knowledge, is the young Marian Evans herself, transmuted into fiction. Maggie repeats her author's childish troubles for she is often in disgrace, considered plain and tiresome, compared unfavourably with her pretty, docile cousin, Lucy, as Marian had been with Chrissey. With Maggie as with her creator the strongest need is the need of being loved, the second the need for more scope than her surroundings provide. Somewhere in herself she feels possibilities that might be realized in a world of less rigid conventions and narrow judgements; she knows instinctively that there must be somewhere, a world of different values in which her qualities would not be despised and, when she runs away to the gypsies, it is in the hope of finding such a world, less cramping to the fullness of her own instinctive life.

With her adoration of her brother, Tom, and her sense of inferiority as a mere girl who can only share his amusements on sufferance, there is also a feeling of superiority, for Maggie is quicker than the stupid Tom and knows it, even while she reveres him for the things which she cannot do and craves for his approval. It is because Tom, disapproving, threatens to tell their father, whose health is failing, that Maggie gives up the stolen meetings with Philip Wakem that are the only break in her restricted life. Later, when Maggie is spending a holiday with Lucy and half-unconsciously steals the love of her recognized admirer, Stephen Guest, the worst of her punishment for the abortive elopment is Tom's anger. The climax of the book is the reconciliation between brother and sister at the moment of death, when both are swept down together by a mass of wreckage in the flooded river. It does not make any difference that Tom is stupid, self-righteous and uncomprehending. He remains to the end the pivot of Maggie's world, exercising that power over her which the lesser but more fully integrated personality so often wields over the characte with so much greater potentialities, but still disorganize

The Mill on the Floss has both the strength and the weakness of an autobiographical novel. There is no more vivid picture in English fiction of the sorrows and sufferings of a child. The world of those early chapters is the world as seen through the eyes of a child. George Eliot used, of course, with some adaptation, the surroundings of her own home, and visitors to the house at Griff can still see the mill, and the Red Deeps where Maggie had the stolen interviews with Philip. By the time that George Eliot wrote *The Mill on the Floss*, she had abandoned her girlish belief that happiness was wrong, and renunciation good for its own sake. Her very life as a writer had depended on her being able to abandon it, but, in her portrait of the young Maggie, she allows no mature nor objective judgement to qualify the identification. The portrait gains in freshness and intensity as much as it loses in proportion.

The second half of *The Mill on the Floss* is less closely autobiographical. Stephen Guest has often been criticized as unworthy of Maggie and unlikely to attract her love. Certainly he is only seen from outside, and is a local dandy, a vain complacent, trivial young man, but Maggie, like so many people with greater powers of feeling, is slow in coming to emotional maturity. She has led a starved life teaching in a girls' school. Stephen is young, gay, and handsome. George Eliot does convey, although it was not possible for a novelist in Victorian England to say it, that what sprang up between them was sexual feeling. Maggie, like her creator, is avid for love. Less fortunate than her creator, she moves in a world where there is no one of her own calibre. She loves the most attractive man she knows, as soon as he breaks down her resistance by showing a preference for her. A novelist writing to-day would probably be aware that there must have been some satisfaction as well as other feelings in taking Stephen from Lucy, the girl who had been held up to her as a model in her childhood as Chrissey had to Marian. George Eliot's high-mindedness and the comparative innocence of her period leaves these undercurrents unexplored. Maggie is all remorse about Lucy, Lucy all gentle forgiveness. Lucy is an idealized portrait but, as with Dinah Morris, George Eliot succeeds in giving to what might have been simply an intolerable prig a sweetness that makes her bearable.

The Mill on the Floss does not depend only on Maggie and her story. It has a superb setting of English family life, narrated as always by George Eliot with humour and shrewd observation. Mrs Tulliver is a woman in herself of little personality, but, as the representative of the Dodson family, she has an authority which the more lively Mr Tulliver resents but cannot always resist. Aunt Glegg is the embodiment of these always-right Dodsons. Bullying her husband and her sisters, exacting the full measure of respect due to her from younger relatives, touchy, arrogant, quick tempered, she refuses to receive Mr Tulliver when he offends her, but is resolute in leaving her will unaltered, for people must not be able to say after she is dead that she did not do right by her sister's children. She is the harshest critic of Maggie as she grows up, but when Maggie is disgraced in the eyes of their world, it is Aunt Glegg who offers her a home. Not that she needs to, for in this crisis the flabby, poor-spirited Mrs Tulliver stands by her child. The central religion of the Dodson family is that blood is thicker than water. The Dodsons are the very marrow of English middle class of the last century, a tradition that still survives.

A Dodson would not be taxed with the omission of anything that was becoming, or that belonged to the eternal fitness of things, which was plainly indicated in the practice of the most substantial parishioners and in the family tradition—such as obedience to parents, faithfulness to kindred, industry, rigid honesty, thrift, the thorough scouring of wooden and copper utensils, the hoarding of coin likely to disappear from the currency, the production of first rate commodities for market, the general preference for whatever is home-made.

Silas Marner
Adam Bede and *The Mill on the Floss* were novels filled

with their author's direct experience. Her father and mother, her own childhood, the aspirations of her youth, her relationships with her brother, her devotion to Miss Lewis provided a good deal of the material, translated, of course, since she was always a novelist, into fiction. In her three last novels she was to move further away from immediate experience and to create in the truth of that experience different worlds. Between the early novels and the later ones come two interim books, very different from each other, both marking an extension of imagination. They were *Silas Marner*, and her only historical novel, *Romola*.

Silas Marner (1861), the shortest and in form the most perfect of all George Eliot's novels, is really a fairy tale expressed in everyday village life. As in so many fairy tales, the focal point is gold, the gold which Marner, the old, epileptic weaver hoards under the stone in his cottage, and which is stolen from him by Dunstan Cass, the Squire's dissolute son. On Christmas Eve, the very season of magic gifts, while the whole neighbourhood is dancing and feasting at the Squire's house, the solitary, half-blind weaver, recovering from one of his fits, sees something on the stone floor of his cottage which may be his lost gold come back to him. Still partly dazed from the epileptic attack, he puts out his hand and touches the living gold of a child's hair. There follows the redemption by love. Silas, whose feelings have atrophied while his only object was to make money and save it, now begins a new life as the father of an adopted child.

The child is the link with the other half of the story, the fortunes of the Cass family. Dunstan's bones whiten undiscovered in the Stone Pit. Godfrey is set free on that Christmas Eve to court and marry Nancy Lammeter, free from the burden of a young man's rash marriage, for the child who wandered into Silas Marner's hut had not come there alone, but had tottered toward the light of his fire from the side of a woman who was found lying dead at his doorway in the snow.

Silas Marner is so complete a work of art that the reader feels no incongruity between the romantic tale and its realistic setting. Is it probable that even a near-sighted man would mistake gold hair for gold coins? It does not much matter. This most charming of George Eliot's novels has the quality of a legend, the kind of story that would be handed down in the village for years afterwards. It is the perfect Christmas story. The conversation of the men in the Rainbow Inn has often been admired for its veracity and liveliness. The weaknesses of the two Cass brothers are admirably described. Nancy Lammeter is another of those young women whose prettiness George Eliot conveys so vividly—although it has been said of her that she is often hard on them. She, who had no doubt suffered a good deal from believing herself ugly, had an acute sense of feminine beauty. There is a fairy tale quality again in the preparations for the party in the Squire's house, the dresses of silvery twilled silk lifted from the clean, rustling paper, the necklace of coral clasped round Miss Nancy's white neck. It is not a fairy tale that ends in complete happiness all round, for Godfrey has to continue to suffer his childlessness, the penalty for distrusting Nancy's generosity, and for disowning his child for eighteen years. Perhaps *Silas Marner* is the best introduction to George Eliot, certainly for a young reader, and it is the most shapely of all her novels.

Romola

Silas Marner, for all its real picture of village life, is an excursion into fantasy. *Romola* (1863), also a spring away from memories of George Eliot's youth, goes to a world which she could only know from books, and by the patient reconstruction of a learned and historically conscious traveller. It is a full, elaborately documented story of Florence in the time of Savonarola. 'It is', says Doctor Leavis, 'the work of a gifted mind but of a mind misusing itself.' To most of her admirers it is the least readable of all her novels. The characters, weighed down by their historical trappings, too deliberately and carefully established in their period, move heavily, and have much less vitality than her men and women of the English midlands. George Eliot put more work into *Romola* than into any other novel. She herself said that she began the book a young women, and finished it an old one.

Romola, the noble and beautiful Florentine girl, is, like Maggie Tulliver, a self-portrait, in some ways more like her author, for she is the only one of her notable women to whom George Eliot attempted to give her own intellectual equipment. Tito, the Greek, who marries Romola and afterwards turns against her, is another and meaner version of Arthur Donnithorne. He has deceived Tessa, an ignorant young *contadina*, with a ceremony of mock marriage, and she innocently believes the children whom she bears him to be legitimate, one day to be publicly acknowledged by their father, whose secret appearances and disappearances she hardly dreams of questioning. When Tito has succumbed to the avenger, who has been dogging him throughout the book, Romola, who has no child, takes in Tessa and the children and shelters them. The story is played out against the full historical background, the arrival of the French under Charles VIII, the struggle between the followers of the Medici and the popular party, the trial and execution of Savonarola.

Perhaps one of the things that make *Romola* so much less lively and readable than George Eliot's other novels is that she is denying herself the use of one of her greatest gifts, her use of ordinary conversation. Her men and women of the English midlands live by the pungency and vitality of their speech, whereas Romola and Tito use a carefully manufactured dialogue, meant to represent the speech of their time. Yet even though many admirers of George Eliot find *Romola* difficult to read and have no desire to re-read it, it is still recognizably the work of a great novelist, in scope and breadth, and in humanity and compassion.

Felix Holt

Sometimes a book on which the writer spends great care and labour with only partly successful results acts as a spring-board for the imagination. Certainly after *Romola* George Eliot wrote her three greatest novels. It may be that the historical perspective of *Romola* turned her mind towards the history of her own time. *Felix Holt* (1866) is a political novel although the politics are not the best part of it. It is an uneven book, the plot is involved, depending on legal complications in the inheritance of the Transome estate. The legal business is both tedious and unconvincing, there is something of an outworn tradition in all the farrago of the missing heir, and the interloper turned out. There is a lively and vigorous picture of an election in a country town, but the great strength of the novel lies in the emotional drama of the Transome family.

Mrs Transome, hardened by her unhappy secret; Harold Transome with his carefully planned life, and his always realizable ambitions, his good-tempered selfishness; Jermyn, the coarse-fibred rascal, who is also a good and affectionate husband and father, misusing his trust for the welfare of his family—all these are drawn with the hand of a master. We are skilfully and gradually made aware of the likeness between Harold and Jermyn. The commonplace egotism of Jermyn, tempered by Mrs Transome's keen-edged personality, becomes in their son a hardness veiled by natural geniality. All that is greedy and unprincipled in Jermyn is also greedy and unprincipled in the son, although a different nurture and a wider experience have put a finer glaze on the surface. Mrs Transome, the bitter old woman, realizes that she will get no more real tenderness from her son than from her former lover. Her tragedy is not only that she has implicated both with herself in an impossible situation, but that she is necessary to neither.

Felix Holt is meant to be the foil to Harold and Jermyn. He is the idealized 'working man' of his time, the high-principled reformer who cares nothing for personal advantage and is willing to give his life to the cause of the oppressed. He is determined not to rise out of his own class, but to remain in it as a manual worker and to devote his spare energies to educating the children of his fellow workers. George Eliot was no revolutionary in politics. A gradual improvement in conditions and nurture was her idea of a revolution. She had nothing like the inside knowledge of the hardships of poverty that Mrs Gaskell showed in *Mary Barton*. Perhaps the reason was that the poor whom she really knew were all country people, and poverty is always less bearable in a city. Felix Holt remains an embodiment of an idea, and an idea perceived intellectually from outside, rather than a living person. He is most alive in his relationship with the lovely, lively Esther Lyon. The early scenes between the two when they are falling reluctantly in love and want to conceal it from themselves by sparring are very good indeed. Esther softens into love and tenderness, and although she appreciates luxury and position, and is delighted to find herself able to be at home in the Transome world, she throws it all away for Felix's sake.

As always the novel is remarkable not only for the main theme, but for the humour and veracity of the minor characters. No English novelist, not Dickens himself, is more at home in the public house and the market place. Some of the characters recall those of the earlier novels: Rufus Lyon is again, like Dinah Morris and Mr Tryan, the saintly evangelical, Felix Holt's grumbling but devoted mother recalls Lizbeth Bede, but Esther is no longer a heroine drawn from her author's own self-portrait, and Mrs Transome, Harold, and Jermyn are genuine creations. There is nothing in George Eliot's work more powerful than the tragedy of Mrs Transome. The destiny whose seed was sown so long ago is worked out in the course of the novel with the inevitability of a Greek drama. *Felix Holt* is not one of the best-known or most widely read of George Eliot's novels, probably because the political novel is not popular with English readers, but it is certainly one of the most worth reading.

Middlemarch

Middlemarch (1871-2) is now generally recognized, not only as the full flower of George Eliot's genius, but as one of the finest novels in the English language. Its subtitle is *A Study of Provincial Life*. Its scene is a country town in the Midlands, and the big houses around the town. Its theme, as Gerald Bullett has said in his book on George Eliot, is 'the diversity of provincial manners and the significance of ordinary lives'.

Its several strands are connected by the slight and apparently casual threads which link up human lives. As in nearly every great novel, there is more than one story. There is the story of Dorothea Brooke, an ardent girl, unsatisfied by the idle country-house life in which she has been brought up. Like Maggie Tulliver, like the young Marian Evans, she is conscious of powers yearning for development, and of an intensity that sets her apart from the household in which she lives, even from her sister, Celia, the natural young woman, who is half afraid of Dorothea's superiority, and half amused at 'Dodo's notions'. It is inevitable that Celia, whose lighter personality has matured earlier, should marry the robust and conventional Sir James Chettam, while Dorothea marries the elderly scholar, Casaubon. She dreams of devoting her life to helping him with his work, only to discover that this great work is an occupation that offers him a retreat from life, a dreary hotch-potch of other men's ideas, endlessly compiled for a book that will never be written and could have no value if it were. Apart from the disillusionment about Casaubon's work, Dorothea suffers the natural disappointment of a vigorous young woman married to a man prematurely old in whom feeling has long since atrophied, although he has enough jealousy to see before Dorothea is aware of it the dawning love between her and his cousin, the artist, Will Ladislaw.

Ladislaw is one of the links with the story of Lydgate, the young doctor who comes to Middlemarch full of faith in himself and in the work, scientific and practical, that he means to do. He is a parallel with Dorothea, for he too marries somebody who is the negation to all his aspirations. Rosamund Vincy, the daughter of a comfortable, unpretentious family, has been educated out of homeliness and into gentility. Completely self-centred, she is hardly aware of Lydgate as a person; she sees him as an opportunity of climbing out of the tradesmen's world in which she was born, into professional and county society. Her values are incomprehensible to him as his are to her, but her blinkered obstinacy prevails, and his ambitions are caught up in a net of debts incurred to satisfy his wife's idea of happiness. He loses the fine edge of his integrity, and incurs suspicion of deep disgrace from which he is never wholly cleared except in the opinion of his nearest friends. He leaves Middlemarch to make what life he can, a successful one, since he is an able man, but with an incompatible wife, and disappointed hopes.

It is easier to sympathize with him in his tragic self-betrayal than with Bulstrode, whose ostentatious virtue and high reputation in Middlemarch are based on a shabby fraud at the expense of a widow and her child. Yet Bulstrode, because he is handled with profound compassion, moves the reader. One of the most poignant passages in the book is the account of his wife's discovery that the husband whom she has always revered has cheated over his first wife's estate, and that his disgrace is known in Middlemarch. It is the end of all her happiness and pride. Obeying an instinct which she cannot articulate, she lingers in her bedroom, taking off her ornaments and changing her elaborate hair-dressing for a plain one, putting on a black dress, mourning for the life of respect and importance she has shared with him. Going downstairs at last she sees him in his chair, looking withered and shrunken. She puts a hand on his shoulder, saying gently, 'Look up, Nicholas' so that he bursts into tears and without question or answer they weep side by side.

George Eliot's novels have abounded in the saints of the Evangelical Movement, but in Bulstrode she presents another of the characters whom the Movement seemed to foster, the man who combines a steady and not always scrupulous pursuit of profit and success with a religion which is always on his lips but in a separate compartment of his heart. 'It was a principle with Mr Bulstrode to gain as much power as possible that he might use it for the glory of God. He went through a great deal of spiritual conflict and inward argument in order to adjust his motives and make clear to himself what God's glory required.'

In contrast to Lydgate and Bulstrode, the man of unshakeable integrity is Caleb Garth, the land agent, another version of George Eliot's father, an older and more human Adam Bede; his daughter, Mary, in her sturdy sense and loyalty is the one hope of stability for Fred Vincy, spoiled like his sister Rosamond, but not ruined, because unlike her, he has a warm heart. Fred has been nearly destroyed by vain expectations. Another plot, which might almost be the plot of a detective novel, is focused on Stone Court, where the rich old Featherstone lies dying, watched faithfully by Mary Garth, and hungrily by all those who could hope to benefit by his death.

All these strands are woven into a pattern of that varied scene of provincial life which George Eliot knew so much better than any other woman writer of her century. She was at ease in the billiard room of the public house, in the Rectory parlour, at the committee meeting, and in the drawing-room of the country house. Dorothea Brooke is a woman, like her creator, of exceptional quality, but everyone else in the book is of average stature. They are people of moderate gifts and mixed faults and virtues, to whom George Eliot has given significance by her respect for them as human beings and by her profound sympathy and compassion. Even when she is writing of how Rosamond

Vincy's shallow egotism destroys her husband, she sees the disappointing marriage, too, through Rosamond's eyes, and shows that she, too, in her limited way, is a feeling and suffering human being. Fred Vincy is an unsatisfactory young scapegoat to such judges as Mrs Garth and his father, but how sympathetically, and also with what humour, George Eliot draws his own young impatience with the people who grudge him a bit of fun, and are for ever 'at him' about the serious purposes of life.

Deeply concerned, like all George Eliot's novels, with the serious purposes of life, *Middlemarch* is also enlivened all the time by humour. It is the funniest of all her books. Even Dorothea, with whom she obviously identifies herself, she sees sometimes through the amused eyes of Celia.

Occasionally the humour fails, as in some of the scenes between Dorothea and Will Ladislaw, the only character in the book who never for an instant comes to life, but everywhere it provides the savour in this long sober chronicle of ordinary life, which leaves the reader with the conviction that lives after all are never ordinary when presented by an author who feels them deeply and can discern at least a part of their pattern.

Daniel Deronda

Daniel Deronda (1876), George Eliot's last novel, draws much less on her early knowledge of farm and village. Its scene is laid in country houses, in London and abroad.

There are two main stories: the story of Gwendolen Harleth, a brilliantly pretty, spirited, self-absorbed girl, with a doting mother and subdued half sisters, and the story of a young Jewess, Mirah, who comes to England to find her long lost mother and brother; Mirah, gentle and affectionate, is a complete foil for Gwendolen.

The link between the two stories is Daniel Deronda himself, the adopted son of an English country gentleman, Sir Hugo Mallinger, who has brought him up in ignorance of his parentage. Daniel supposes himself and is supposed to be Sir Hugo's illegitimate son. He is a serious young man with great integrity and with a natural authority which affects most of those who come near him.

Gwendolen's fortunes are linked with Deronda in the dramatic opening scene, when he is idly watching the gambling in the Casino at a French watering-place, and notices a beautiful girl who stakes her last guinea and loses. Next morning Deronda happens to see her going into a pawn shop. When she has come out he enters and buys the turquoise necklace which she has just sold. He returns it to her with an unsigned note of gentle reproach. Gwendolen finds out who wrote the note and from that day Daniel Deronda becomes in her mind a mentor whose approval she craves.

At their home of Offendene in England Gwendolen's mother and half sisters are facing ruin from the failure of their investments. Before going abroad Gwendolen had refused an offer of marriage from Grandcourt, the great man of the neighbourhood. She did not love him but he could have given her much that she wanted; she would probably have accepted him, but she discovered that he already had four children by a woman whom he had promised to marry.

When Gwendolen returns to Offendene Grandcourt again proposes to her. She has to choose between this splendid marriage and a humble post as a governess. She knows that Grandcourt is hard and selfish, but, confident in her young beauty, she believes that she will easily manage him. When she discovers that Grandcourt's inbuilt egotism is too much for her she turns for comfort to Deronda, whom she often meets in London society. Grandcourt perceives what Gwendolen does not know, that she is in love with Deronda and sweeps her off on a Mediterranean yachting cruise.

Deronda's life is moving in another direction, towards Mirah, whom he saves from suicide and towards her brother,

Ezra Mordecai, who turns out to be a man of great emotional and intellectual power, but dying of consumption. He implores Deronda to carry on his work and help to restore the Jews to their own country.

Sir Hugo send Deronda out to Genoa to see his dying mother, who proves to have been a famous Jewish singer and who reveals to him that his father was a Jew.

Gwendolen and Grandcourt are also in Genoa. She is miserable, having discovered on this holiday the full extent of her husband's sadism. When they are out sailing Grandcourt is swept overboard; Gwendolen, paralysed by shock and conflict of feeling, is slow in throwing the rope to him. A minute later she desperately jumps in and tries to save him. She is rescued but Grandcourt is drowned. To Deronda she confesses that she feels herself a murderess. She was too late with the rope because 'I saw my wish outside me'.

Deronda tries to comfort her, but the discovery of his Jewish birth turns him finally towards Mirah and the service of his own people. Gwendolen is left desolate with nothing but the hope that she may in time become the kind of woman that Deronda would wish her to be.

Nothing that George Eliot wrote is more powerful than this study of Gwendolen Harleth. The change from the wilful, glowing girl into the bullied wife is superbly handled. George Eliot does not attempt to disguise Gwendolen's murderous feelings towards Grandcourt. That cry 'I saw my wish outside me', ushers in the changed attitude towards human nature that divides the novels of this century from those of the last. *Daniel Deronda* is a great novel which combines the modern sense of complexity of character with the fullness and richness of Victorian fiction.

III. CONCLUSION

Daniel Deronda was George Eliot's last novel. It is by her novels alone that she lives. She wrote a number of short stories, of which the most remarkable is 'The Lifted Veil', a good deal of pedestrian poetry, including a long dramatic poem, *The Spanish Gypsy*, and a book of satirical essays called *Impressions of Theophrastus Such*. All her work was written during the twenty-three years of her life with George Lewes. In 1878, two years after the publication of *Daniel Deronda*, Lewes died.

It was a mortal blow to George Eliot, who lived only two years after him. The end of her story is a strange one. For weeks after Lewes's death she shut herself up and remained in a stupor of despair, seeing no one. The first friend she did care to see was John Walter Cross, the son of a London merchant, one of the many intelligent young men who had frequented the house near Regent's Park. Cross was at that time thirty-nine and George Eliot sixty. He had just lost his mother, to whom he was devoted, and no doubt he turned unconsciously to George Eliot to fill her place, as she turned to him in a desperate search for comfort. They were constantly together, and on 6 May 1880 they were married.

George Eliot called the astonishing marriage 'a blessing falling to me beyond my share'. It has been conjectured that it was a relief to her conscience to find herself at last a married woman. It seems more likely that she, for whom George Lewes's love had been life itself, was snatching desperately at any comfort to relieve the agony of loneliness and deprivation. There was no time to see how the strange marriage would work. Cross seems to have been devoted to Marian. After her death he compiled the first biography from her letters and journals. No doubt his affection and his company gave Marian some comfort. Her nature was deeply loving and it had become a necessity to her to have someone to love, and to be protected and cherished. But the loss of Lewes had been a blow too deep for recovery. In December 1880, six months after her marriage, she died.

In a review of *Felix Holt*, published soon after its appearance, Henry James summed up George Eliot's work. He spoke of her, 'closely wedded talents and foibles', and said that her plots are artificial and her conclusions weak. In compensation for these defects, we have the broad array of rich accomplishments. First the firm and elaborate delineation of individual character. Then that extension of human sympathy, that easy understanding of character at large. That familiarity with man from which a novelist draws his real inspiration, to which he owes it that, firm locked in the most rigid prose, he is still more or less a poet. George Eliot's humanity colours all her other gifts.

She was not a writer who in her lifetime had to struggle for recognition. From the publication of her first book, she was acknowledged by her peers, and these included Dickens and Thackeray. Her career was one of unbroken success and, in spite of her moods of diffidence and self distrust, she knew herself to be an important novelist.

After her death her reputation seemed for a time to be obscured. No one really interested in the English novel could ignore her, but many people who did not read her had an idea of her as a governessy blue-stocking, a turgid, out-of-date Victorian. Lately a more general interest in her work has revived, and the sound and affectionate studies by Gerald Bullett and by Joan Bennett, Dr Leavis's critical estimate, T. W. J. Harvey's study as well as Gordon Haight's full biography, and the television versions of her novels have stimulated a more just and also a more general appreciation of her superb gifts.

It is now more than a hundred years since the publication of *Scenes of Clerical Life*. During that time a change has taken place in the attitude of both novelists and their readers to the characters in a novel. To say that moral judgement in the novelist and in the reader has disappeared would be an exaggeration, for there is no one civilized enough to read a book who has not some moral standard to which he expects himself, and still more other people to conform, and, even if he does not know it, he applies this in fiction as in life. Moreover, those standards in Western civilization are impregnated with the Christian tradition, and with values accepted over hundreds of years. But moral judgement, although nearly always there, is in the background, often unacknowledged, and it depends far more now on individual taste in life and less on agreed standards.

What has very nearly departed from the novel and from the reader of the novel, is moral concern. The modern novelist wishes to present a picture of life from some angle. The reader wishes to see what that particular facet of life is like. He does not feel distressed if the characters in a novel behave badly. His great interest is to see how and why they behave badly. On the whole neither the writer nor the reader feel moral concern for the characters, they feel a more objective interest. Moral concern for her characters was the very essence of George Eliot. 'Is he, or she, going to manage to be noble or not?' is the real plot of her novels. Sometimes her ideas of nobility are unacceptable to one kind of modern reader, who has learnt that unselfishness can be a masochism, and sometimes forgets that it can also be love, who is more afraid of priggishness than of homicide, insanity, or perversion. But the choice between living by one's own best or second best values is still universal. It is the urgency of that choice that creates the tension in George Eliot's work, and without tension there is no great novel.

There is no doubt whatever that George Eliot is a great novelist. Her awareness of life is both wide and deep. She is one of the most intellectual of English novelists, but with her intellectual power goes no tinge of contempt, nothing that dries up her sympathy with average men and women. She uses a mind nourished by philosophy and learning to express the significance of ordinary lives. With that 'firm and elaborate delineation of individual character' of which Henry James spoke, is combined a genius for bringing each character to life, not only as an individual but as part of the social pattern. Her vision is whole. For her there is no division between the inner and outer life, between the profound emotion, the agonizing spiritual conflict, and the bargain in the lawyer's office, the election brawl, the gossip in farm kitchen or tap room. All is unified by her deep-rooted love of humanity. Beneath all her faithful and often humorous rendering of its meannesses and absurdities lies her sense of its potential grandeur.

She is vividly aware of its humour. Infinitely pompous and solemn in her private correspondence, she shows in all her novels the shrewd and racy humour of an old country-woman, which only breaks down when she is handling one of her idealized characters or one of those too closely identified with herself. Her dialogue is nearly always masterly. The tirades of her vigorous older women, the talk of men idling or working together, have the veracity of simple poetry, and reveal the nature of the speakers more effectively than any description.

George Eliot's particular contribution to the English novel is that she left it aware of character on a very much deeper level. Her analysis of motive is penetrating, and she has more understanding than any English novelist writing before Freud of the undercurrents of mind and heart. Because her human beings are more complicated and more mixed than those of the novelists who preceded her, they are nearer to the truth of human nature. This penetration is not only of the intellect, it is born of a harmony between mind and feeling, illuminated by compassion and love for humanity. In her best work there is a depth and reality that no English novelist has surpassed, nor can any of them surpass her in her power of taking the reader into her created world.

GEORGE ELIOT

A Select Bibliography

(Place of publication London, unless stated otherwise. Detailed biblio-
graphical information will also be found in the appropriate volumes
of *The Cambridge Bibliography of English Literature*.)

Bibliography:

A BIBLIOGRAPHY OF THE FIRST EDITIONS OF BOOKS OF GEORGE ELIOT,
by P. H. Muir
—contributed to the *Bookman's Journal* Supplement, 1927–8.
VICTORIAN LADY NOVELISTS: GEORGE ELIOT, by M. L. Parrish; New
York (1933)
—first editions of George Eliot formerly in the Library of M. L.
Parrish and now in Princetown University, expertly described and
annotated by their late owner.

Collected Editions:

THE NOVELS, 6 vols; Edinburgh (1867–78).
THE WORKS, 20 vols; Edinburgh (1878–80)
—the Cabinet edition.
THE COMPLETE POETICAL WORKS; New York (1888).
THE COMPLETE POEMS, ed. M. Browne; Boston, Mass. (1888).
THE WORKS, 12 vols; Edinburgh (1901–3)
—the Warwick edition.
THE WORKS, 21 vols (1908–11).
THE GEORGE ELIOT LETTERS, ed. G. S. Haight, 7 vols; London, New
Haven (1954–5).

Separate Works:

THE LIFE OF JESUS CRITICALLY EXAMINED, by D. F. Strauss. Translated
from the fourth German edition by Marian Evans, 3 vols (1846)
—begun by Mrs C. Hennell and completed by Marian Evans (i.e.,
G. Eliot).
THE ESSENCE OF CHRISTIANITY, by L. Feuerbach. Translated from the
second German edition by Marian Evans (1854).
SCENES OF CLERICAL LIFE, 2 vols; Edinburgh (1858). *Novel*
ADAM BEDE, 3 vols; Edinburgh (1859). *Novel*
THE MILL ON THE FLOSS, 3 vols; Edinburgh (1860). *Novel*
SILAS MARNER: The Weaver of Raveloe; Edinburgh (1861). *Novel*

ROMOLA, 3 vols (1863). *Novel*
FELIX HOLT, THE RADICAL, 3 vols; Edinburgh (1866). *Novel*
THE SPANISH GYPSY: A Poem; Edinburgh (1868).
HOW LISA LOVED THE KING; Boston, Mass. (1869). *Verse*
MIDDLEMARCH: A Study of Provincial Life, 4 vols; Edinburgh (1871–2). *Novel*
THE LEGEND OF JUBAL, AND OTHER POEMS; Edinburgh (1874).
DANIEL DERONDA, 4 vols; Edinburgh (1876). *Novel*
IMPRESSIONS OF THEOPHRASTUS SUCH; Edinburgh (1879). *Essays*
ESSAYS AND LEAVES FROM A NOTE-BOOK, ed. C. L. Lewes; Edinburgh (1884).
EARLY ESSAYS (1919)
—privately printed.

Letters:

GEORGE ELIOT'S LIFE AS RELATED IN HER LETTERS AND JOURNALS, arranged and edited by her husband, J. W. Cross, 3 vols; Edinburgh (1885).
LETTERS TO ELMA STUART, 1872–80, ed. R. Stuart (1909).
LETTERS, sel. R. Brimley Johnson (1926).
GEORGE ELIOT'S FAMILY LIFE AND LETTERS, by A. Paterson (1928).
THE GEORGE ELIOT LETTERS, ed. G. S. Haight, 7 vols; London, New Haven (1954–5).

Some Critical and Biographical Studies:

GEORGE ELIOT IN DERBYSHIRE, by Guy Roslyn [i.e. Joshua Hatton] (1876).
GEORGE ELIOT AND JUDAISM, by D. Kaufmann; Edinburgh (1877).
THE ETHICS OF GEORGE ELIOT'S WORKS, by J. C. Brown; Edinburgh (1879).
GEORGE ELIOT, by W. Morgan (1881).
GEORGE ELIOT, by M. Blind (1883).
GEORGE ELIOT: A Critical Study of Her Life, Writings and Philosophy, by G. W. Cooke (1883).
GEORGE ELIOT'S POETRY AND OTHER STUDIES, by R. E. Cleveland (1885).
GEORGE ELIOT: Thoughts upon Her Life, Her Books and Herself, by M. Lonsdale (1886).
LIFE OF GEORGE ELIOT, by O. Browning (1890).
GEORGE ELIOT, by Sir L. Stephen (1902)
—in the *English Men of Letters* Series.
GEORGE ELIOT, by C. L. Thomson (1901).

GEORGE ELIOT: Scenes and People in Her Novels, by C. S. Olcott; New York (1910).

THE INNER LIFE OF GEORGE ELIOT, by C. Gardner (1912).

THE EARLY LIFE OF GEORGE ELIOT, by M. H. Deakin; Manchester (1913).

GEORGE ELIOT AND THOMAS HARDY, by L. W. Berle; New York (1917).

NOTES ON THE INFLUENCE OF SIR WALTER SCOTT ON GEORGE ELIOT, by A. J. C.; Edinburgh (1923).

A GEORGE ELIOT DICTIONARY, by I. G. Mudge and M. E. Sears; New York (1924).

THE COMMON READER by V. Woolf (1925)
—contains an essay on George Eliot.

THE HOMES OF GEORGE ELIOT: An Appreciative Commenatry on Her Characteristics and Philosophy, by A. L. Summers (1926).

GEORGE ELIOT AND HER TIMES: A Victorian Study, by E. S. Haldane (1927).

GEORGE ELIOT'S FAMILY LIFE AND LETTERS, by A. Paterson (1928).

GEORGE ELIOT, by J. L. May (1930).

LA VIE DE GEORGE ELIOT, by E. and G. Romieu; Paris (1930)
—English translation by B. W. Downs, 1932.

GEORGE LEWES AND GEORGE ELIOT, by A. T. Kitchel; New York (1933).

EARLY VICTORIAN NOVELISTS, by Lord David Cecil (1934)
—contains an essay on George Eliot.

GEORGE ELIOT: A Biography, by B. C. Williams; New York (1936).

MARIAN: The Life of George Eliot, by S. Dewes (1939).

GEORGE ELIOT: Her Life and Books, by G. Bullett (1947).

GEORGE ELIOT: Her Mind and Her Art, by J. Bennett; Cambridge (1948).

THE GREAT TRADITION, by F. R. Leavis (1948)
—contains an important critical study of George Eliot.

NINETEENTH CENTURY STUDIES, by B. Willey (1949)
—contains a section on George Eliot.

GEORGE ELIOT, by R. Speaight (1954)
—new edition, 1968.

THE NOVELS OF GEORGE ELIOT: A Study in Form, by B. Hardy (1959).

GEORGE ELIOT THE WOMAN, by M. Crompton (1960).

THE ART OF GEORGE ELIOT, by W. J. Harvey (1961).

MIDDLEMARCH FROM NOTEBOOK TO NOVEL: A Study of George Eliot's creative method, by J. Beaty; Urbana (1960).

ENGLISH NOVEL: Form and Function, by D. Van Ghent. (1961).

GEORGE ELIOT, by W. Allen (1965).

A CENTURY OF GEORGE ELIOT CRITICISM, ed. G. S. Haight; Boston, Mass. (1965).

THE TRUTHTELLERS: Jane Austen, George Eliot, D. H. Lawrence, by L. Lerner (1967).

GEORGE ELIOT IN FRANCE: A French Appraisal of George Eliot's Writings, 1858–1960, by J. P. Couch; Chapel Hill, North Carolina (1967).

GEORGE ELIOT: A Biography, by G. S. Haight; Oxford (1968).

GEORGE ELIOT: A Biography, by R. Sprague; Philadelphia, London (1968).

GEORGE ELIOT, by I. Adam (1969).

CRITICAL ESSAYS ON GEORGE ELIOT, ed. B. Hardy (1970).

GEORGE ELIOT, ed. A. E. S. Viner (1970).

GEORGE ELIOT: A Collection of Critical Essays, ed. G. R. Creeger; Englewood Cliffs (1970).

GEORGE ELIOT AND JOHN CHAPMAN, by G. S. Haight (1970).

INDEX OF ESSAYS AND PAPERS

(The title in italics refers to the main title of the book.)